LOSE YOUR LIMITS: GROW YOUR BUSINESS

THE 5 KEY SYSTEM TO GO FROM STRUGGLING BUSINESS OWNER TO LIMITLESS ENTREPRENEUR

CHRISTIAN CHASMER
#1 BESTSELLING AUTHOR

WWW.LOSETHELIMITS.COM

For orders, please email: christian@losethelimits.com

"

Lose Your Limits; Grow Your Business should be in every entrepreneur's library. This book gives you the blueprint for business success and does so by going deeper than the typical business books and cutting straight to the root of what's holding most people back: themselves. Highly recommend!"

– HAL ELROD

#1 bestselling author, *The Miracle Morning*

"This book is a powerful mental road map to a limitless life. It will help you identify the obstacles holding you back, and break through to achieve anything and everything you set your mind on. A must read!"

– CHRIS POWELL

Health and fitness trainer, star of ABC's Extreme Weight Loss

"People from every walk of life can learn something from Christian Chasmer's Lose the Limits. The pearls of wisdom shared inside will change the way you think and guide you for years to come".

– THAN MERRILL

Real Estate Investor and Founder of FortuneBuilders.com

"

"This book is not another "pump up" book, but has actual tactics that any entrepreneur can implement to significantly grow their life and business! Highly recommend for all entrepreneurs who want to build their business"

– CHANDLER BOLT
Founder and CEO of Self-Publishing School

"What an outstanding book for any entrepreneur. The takeaways you get from this book will change your life forever if you follow them. Christian is a highly energetic entrepreneur. He is a great student of business with a passion for success. Many books will give you complex concepts, Christian gives you 5 simple concepts to follow which is based on real world experiences not theories. His practical approaches and the worksheets he provides are spot on."

– STEVE ACORN
Founder and CEO of Student Painters/ Young Entrepreneurs Across America

THANKS FOR PURCHASING LOSE YOUR LIMITS!

Just to say thanks for purchasing my book,
I would like to give you the Audiobook version 100% FREE!
Go to this link to download...

LOSETHELIMITS.COM/AUDIOVERSION

THIS BOOK IS FOR...

My role models and mentors who have guided me on this journey called life. *Lose Your Limits: Grow Your Business* is possible because of all of their lessons.

To my mother, godfather, and father who inspired me to be the best version of myself, and to live life with no "what ifs."

LOSE YOUR LIMITS: GROW YOUR BUSINESS

The 5 key system to go from Struggling business owner
to limitless entrepreneur

Christian Chasmer

TABLE OF CONTENTS

ACKNOWLEDGEMENTS 15

PREFACE 17

INTRODUCTION 25

    Five Keys to a New World 29

LIMITING BELIEFS AND ME 33

KEY 1: WHY 39

    First Step – The What 45

    Second Step – The How 48

    Third Step – Major Purpose 50

    Fourth Step –The Why 51

    The what, the how, the why 52

KEY 2: FAILURE 63

    Suzuki 66

    Fear Setting: An Exercise on Accepting Failure 68

KEY 3: HABIT 77

The Fixed Mindset vs. The Growth Mindset   80

Exercise   82

The Morning Routine   83

The Hard Stop   84

Read, Read, Read   86

Integrity   87

The Law of Attraction   88

The Filter   90

KEY 4: PEOPLE 101

Lincoln's "Team of Rivals"   104

KEY 5: GROWTH 111

Growth in Why   117

Growth from Failures   117

Growth in Habits   118

Growth in People   118

NO WHAT IF'S 122

ACKNOWLEDGEMENTS

I want to once again thank my mother who has supported me through every decision I have made.

I'd also like to thank my Godfather, Bob Kassan. He taught me to live life authentically and to, above all things, live life with no "what ifs."

Thank you to Katie Eilbracht for the fantastic cover design, my editor, Chelsea Miller for not holding any punches on the earlier versions of this book, Kevin Martignetti for giving me some great feedback on this book, Mark Pecotta from Launch Boom for helping to create the website and online presence for this launch. You are all amazing people and I am grateful to all of you.

Thank you to my beautiful girlfriend Brittany Swanson for peer editing, helping with cover ideas, and putting up with my general craziness during this whole process.

PREFACE

My go to line when I was a young kid was, "I have the worst luck in the world." I used to literally blame the world for my problems. Bad things would happen to me and I would complain about it to everyone and accept it as "just my life." It was almost as if I thought I deserved the things that were happening to me. As I grew older, I became more aware of these negative thoughts and eventually realized how limiting they were, but nothing changed.

Even as I was becoming successful, these negative thoughts were holding me back from what I truly wanted. It wasn't until I was introduced to the concept of "limiting beliefs" at a business conference for successful "20 something's" that I truly started to reflect on my life. My negative thoughts were much more than simply thoughts. They were limiting beliefs that I had unconsciously adopted into my life and they were really holding me back.

It was then that I started to study my role models: Tony Robbins, Elon Musk, Dwayne Johnson, and the very successful people

I knew in my own life. I started to see patterns in these individuals and chose to adopt the patterns I saw. Very soon after this adoption, my entire life changed. From the inside out, I was at peace with the world. I became the driver of my own destiny. My life goals started to come to fruition, and I was the happiest I have ever been.

On top of happiness, my business ventures started to become successes. My painting company in college grew 4x in size, from $75,000 the first year to $360,000 the second. After college, I started a new division of a college training company and grew that division to $1.2 million in revenue in just ten months. I then struck out on my own with my business partner and we built a real estate development company that in it's second year exceeded $6.5 million in revenue. The business success is great, but the real power behind these lifestyle changes was how they have helped me stay healthy, fulfilled, and connected to the people closest to me while building my businesses.

While I still have a long way to go, I am living proof that these principles work. And that is exactly why I knew I had to share my system. I took the lifestyle changes and boiled them down to the top five most beneficial patterns, which birthed the "five key" system making up this book.

I know the power of limiting beliefs. I have seen them break people down time and time again. I have seen, as we all have, countless people not live up to their potential because they all harbor limiting beliefs. I have heard, "I can't do it" or "I'll never be able to do that" thousands of times in my life, and I get angry every single time I hear it. I see entrepreneurs quit right at the cusp of success because they hit the perceived "wall." I see business owners who are overworked and overstressed all while barely making ends meet. These owners (I used to be one of them) eventually get the limiting belief that this is what entrepreneurship is and either stay in their same position forever or quit and get a job, ultimately staying overworked and overstressed.

If you are like one of these people, this book can inspire you to make a change in your life. *Lose Your Limits: Grow Your Business*, will give you the willpower to break your limiting beliefs and you will be able to live the life you desire, but never thought attainable for yourself. By reading this book, business owners will make the changes they need in their business, even if they are afraid.

When I help someone break down the walls of their limiting beliefs and go for what they want in life and in business, then I did my job. Helping others achieve their maximum potential will not only benefit those individuals, but will also greatly impact our planet. When this book helps one person, and that person helps 2 more people, we can start a chain reaction that helps thousands, even millions of people. Imagine if we had every individual on this planet living up to their maximum potential and contributing to the greater good. What would our world look like? That is what I want to find out.

"

Two roads diverged in a wood,
And I took the one less traveled by, And that
has made all the difference.

— ROBERT FROST

LOSE YOUR LIMITS:
GROW YOUR BUSINESS

INTRODUCTION

As he thinks, so he is;
as he continues to think, so he remains.
- JAMES ALLEN

That voice in your head. The one telling you you're not good enough. The one telling you to quit while you're ahead. That annoying, debilitating, constant humming that is telling you your dreams aren't possible and to just give up. That voice is very dangerous. It stops you from achieving what you want.

You sit there, paralyzed by this voice. You are unable to take action, to go for what you want. You succumb to the siren in your head telling you you're not good enough. You trade dreams for jobs, fulfillment for comfort.

You look to the outside world for validation of this passive lifestyle. You blame the government, the economy, your employees, your parents, your surroundings, and even your genes for your unfulfilled life. You tell yourself this is normal. All the while, that voice gets louder, harder to ignore. Eventually that voice becomes you. You no longer have to hear the voice, because the nasty words are so embedded into your core that you take on the values of that voice. You become a preacher of that voice, instilling its teachings in others, seducing the next generation into believing the same values as that voice.

But that voice isn't you. That voice is fake. The words it tells you, although convincing, are also fake.

That voice is the embodiment of your limiting beliefs and nothing more.

What if you could learn to control these voices and push them away? What if, with work, you could break the chains these limiting beliefs have wrapped around you and live the life you always dreamed? What would you do?

What do you think most people would do?

Probably what they've always done: nothing.

I hate to admit it, but most people would rather do nothing than fight these voices. They'd rather sit idly while time, and life, passes. They are so wrought with fear that they'd rather stay in their comfort zone. They can't imagine anyone wanting to work to live life to the fullest. Most people either act like they don't have any dreams or goals or they act like their dreams and goals are impossible and unrealistic. They think the few people that do live life to the fullest possess mystical powers that propel them to the top.

They look on in awe as the "select" few rise to the top of their industries, make great works of art, and contribute to the greater good.

They believe that people who are always happy and fulfilled must be special, or that they are faking it.

These people do not possess mystical powers, they aren't genetically special, or lucky. All successful and fulfilled people share a common trait: They have learned to quiet that voice inside their head. They refused to be held back by their own negative self-talk. They push forward when that voice says retreat. They keep going when that voice says to quit. They believe in themselves and their cause.

They have learned to break their limiting beliefs, and that is exactly what you will learn to do in this book.

After reading Lose Your Limits: Grow Your Business, you will know exactly how to break the limiting beliefs holding you back from growing your business and ultimately achieving the lifestyle you want. A limiting belief, which is an agreement you have made with yourself that puts a limit on your capabilities, has a drastic impact on the decisions you make in your life and in your business. This book will show you the path to becoming the person that can build your current business to the level you have always dreamed of.

Napoleon Hill sums up limiting beliefs quite eloquently, "There are no limitations to the mind except those we acknowledge."

Some people naturally break down their limiting beliefs, they have a resounding natural ability to do so. To others, their limiting beliefs are imprinted so deeply in their brain, that they actually think it is a fact of life, like gravity or taxes.

In this book, I introduce many examples of limiting beliefs in action. I will also tell you how overcoming them will change your life and business dramatically.

While researching limiting beliefs, I came across five areas of a person's life that were undoubtedly the most critical to master in order to break limiting beliefs and become the person capable of running a successful business. The book is broken up into these five key areas:

1. WHY

2. FAILURE

3. HABIT

4. PEOPLE

5. GROWTH

The strategies mentioned within these five keys have been used by successful, fulfilled individuals throughout time, including the top business people in history.

In addition to unlocking your mind within these five key areas, I will also give you action steps to make these keys actionable. Because let's remember, ideas mean nothing if you don't put them into action.

I have witnessed the power of limiting beliefs throughout my life and have broken my own limiting beliefs to get to where I am. I also have researched this topic for years to get to these five key areas. I have talked with successful entrepreneurs, athletes, and other high achievers all around the country about this very topic and each of them have helped in creating these keys. I have created these principles through my conversations, hours of research, and through what I have seen growing up with my family and in my town. These principles are proven to work.

FIVE KEYS TO A NEW WORLD

It will be a day by day process, but once you finally adopt these five keys, the world will open up to you. Imagine a world where you feel truly free just by living by a few principles that only make you better! You will start to see endless opportunities that you may not have seen before. All of your dreams and goals will now be possible. The goals you have for your business will become attainable. It is an amazing thing to live in a world without limits. By just following the five key system, the entire world around you changes.

Your limiting beliefs have the power to hold you back from the life you want; following these five keys gives you the power to shatter these limiting beliefs and build the business and lifestyle you want.

I promise if you read this book and take to heart these keys, you will see a drastic change in your life – professionally, socially, and physically. You will stop being a victim of your circumstances and finally have the power to take what you want. Those voices within your head won't be able to hold you back. They won't paralyze you and nothing will be able to stop you.

So, I call you to action. It is pivotal to shed those limiting beliefs holding you back. There are two types of people in this world: people that wait for things to happen and people that make things happen. I urge you to take the road less traveled, break your limiting beliefs, implement these systems, and take control of your life. That starts today. Hold yourself accountable, read this book, and change your life.

LIMITING BELIEFS
AND ME

"

Two roads diverged in a wood, and I –
I took the one less traveled by, And that has
made all the difference.
- ROBERT FROST

I had a very interesting childhood. Growing up, I felt like a very lucky kid. My parents loved me and showed it. I daresay I was kind of spoiled. My mom did a great job sheltering me from the realities of our world. It wasn't until I was twelve years old that I realized how different my childhood was from the norm.

I grew up on welfare, in a family where not one person had ever gone to college. I went to a high school where out of about 260 graduates in my class, maybe 40 went away to college despite having a great education system. Many people get stuck there, they think that it is the only place in the world. Many of them fall to peer pressure and become drug addicts or criminals. They create a limiting belief in their mind that living in that town and being a criminal is all they deserve.

I could have easily just accepted that this was going to be my future. But something deep inside me never agreed with that, and my mother would have probably kicked my ass.

I knew that I was going to achieve more, experience more. I earned an academic scholarship and went away to The University of South Carolina.

At the start of school I came in with the attitude that I was not going to be content with being mediocre. However, I soon got absorbed in typical freshman year shenanigans. I was, after all at an SEC school with SEC tailgates. I partied a lot and lost sight of what I wanted in life. I still earned good grades but I did nothing else to progress my future. I actually started to build limiting beliefs doubting my aspirations and goals in life.

It wasn't until I shattered my ankle being a drunken 19 year old that I started to make a change. I couldn't walk for four months, which allowed for a lot of reflection. After deep moments of building limiting beliefs and depression, I had an epiphany: I was better than where I was at that time.

A change in my life happened from that period on. During junior year in college, I joined the best internship on campus and had the unique opportunity to run my own painting business, which scared the hell out of me.

I ran a $73,000 business as a 20 year old and won the "Performance Under Pressure" award with the company. I actually had to fire all of my employees and train all new ones in the middle of the season, which is almost unheard of. I was asked by this company to come back and teach others how to be just as successful while running my own team again. As a consultant, coach, and manager, my team of five college students produced $365,000 in revenue in just three months, and I won the "Executive of the Year" award.

At 22 years old, I moved to Boston and started a division of the same company I worked for in college. My partner and I built the new division to $1.2 million in revenue in ten months. After that season we decided to leave that business and put all of our money into starting a real estate development company, CC Solutions. We quit our job, bought a triplex, and started CC Solutions in the same week. It was a pretty crazy time for us.

But all that success did not come without hardship. We struggled for months getting CC Solutions off the ground. Limiting beliefs began to creep into my mind. Maybe we weren't good enough? Maybe we were ignorant to start a business at 23 years old?

We continued to push on as I unknowingly used the keys described below to work through these limiting beliefs. We survived a turbulent first year and in our second year, the company earned $6.5 million in revenue.

There were a lot of roadblocks, failures (almost going bankrupt) and obstacles along the way. But I didn't let the voices in my head stop me from pursuing my dreams. I didn't let my limiting beliefs paralyze me. Though I still struggle and have doubts, I am living an extremely fulfilled life, and it is all because I broke my limiting beliefs (and my ankle) and pushed my limits further than I ever thought possible.

I didn't know it at the time, but I was focusing on the five key areas to break my limiting beliefs and drastically better my life. From the point I shattered my ankle on, I made incremental steps to be the person I wanted to be. In this book, I will show you the five keys that literally saved my life.

"Most great people have attained their greatest success just one step beyond their greatest failure."
- NAPOLEON HILL

KEY 1: WHY

"

Once you know what you're destined for,
failure becomes impossible.
- FRANK MAGUIRE

Why do you want the things you desire? Why do you put in all those hard hours of work? Why do you want to grow your business? Why do you care so much? Why do you even get out of bed in the morning?

You have a hard time answering these questions well. And that's how I can tell you have a hard time staying motivated when the going gets tough. Unfortunately, you have the most susceptible personality type for limiting beliefs.

But, I can help you answer these questions. This is the first key to breaking your limiting beliefs. You need to know your "why".

Robert Kioyosaki says, "You must find a reason greater than reality." This sounds simple at first, but it is harder than you think to find the true reason why behind the things you do.

Everyone knows <u>what</u> they're doing in life, but very few know <u>why</u> they are doing it. Think about the millions of business owners that go through the motions of everyday life. They clock in, clock out, go home, watch Netflix, and then go to bed. Wash, rinse, repeat.

You just go through the motions of life without knowing your true purpose. Of course with this "wash, rinse, repeat" mindset you don't have motivation. Why would you?

Many "entrepreneurs" jump at a chance to start a company without really knowing why they are starting the type of business they are starting. My guess is you did the same thing.

This "entrepreneur" then quits when the going gets tough. And why not? If they don't know why they're doing something, why would they stick around when things get hard? This is why the small business failure rate in the first four years of operation is 82%.

The wash, rinse, repeat business owner and the "new entrepreneur" suffer from the same problem: a clear lack of "why."

REAL TALK

Let's take John Smith. John works at a factory where he makes widgets. He has a quota that he has to hit. That quota is 20 widgets a day. Day after day he makes these widgets. He doesn't really know what they do, but the job pays. One day his boss comes in and tells John he needs to now make 25 a day. John is angry about this change. He already works hard and doesn't see why his boss randomly hiked his quota. John begrudgingly hits his new quota. John does not take any pride in his work and when people ask him what he does, he quickly tells them then changes the topic.

John is an average worker at the plant. He always hears stories about the top widget maker at a different plant. Her name is Jane. Jane regularly makes 40-50 widgets a day. John cannot fathom what makes Jane work so hard just to make widgets. What is Jane's secret you ask? Well Jane found out that those widgets are used in early detection devices to detect cancer. Each widget Jane makes saves a human life. Jane works so hard because she knows why she is doing what she is doing. In reality, both John and Jane are saving lives, but Jane is much more motivated and fulfilled in her job because she knows the why behind the what.

In life, it is rarely about the what, but the why.

When you don't know your why, you are more prone to anxiety and/or depression because you don't know where you should be heading. You have no direction.

In my college years, I would frequently get anxious. Every time I needed to make a decision I would get this feeling. I started to get anxious during work and even while hanging out with friends.

I started to reflect on why I was feeling this way. I had to be brutally honest with myself to come to the real reason. It was because I did not know what I should really be doing. I wasn't clear on my purpose and why, which caused me to be anxious about my decisions because I didn't know if they aligned with the path I should be taking. How bad is that? I wasn't anxious because I was making wrong decisions, I was anxious because I did not know if I was making wrong or right decisions. So either way, I was anxious and not happy.

Until you get certain about what you want and why you want it, you flounder. You become anxious. You get analysis paralysis. You do nothing.

You need to be certain about what path you want to take before you can make the decisions that get yourself on that path.

There is nothing more powerful than a person with certainty in their why.

Sharon Lechter and Greg Reid, authors of the business allegory *Three Feet From Gold*, describe this phenomenon as "The Knowing." They have found that every successful person has a cause greater than themselves and does not just believe they will be successful – they know they will be. They know within their bones that they will achieve what they want. It is not about the how, but the why.

Every great person throughout history accomplished great things because they had a clearly defined why.

Martin Luther King shared his "why" in front of a quarter of a million people on August 28th, 1963 on the steps of the Lincoln Memorial:

> *I say to you today, my friends, so even though we face the difficulties of today and tomorrow, I still have a dream. It is a dream deeply rooted in the American dream.*
>
> *I have a dream that one day this nation will rise up and live out the true meaning of its creed: 'We hold these truths to be self-evident: that all men are created equal.'*
>
> *I have a dream that one day on the red hills of Georgia the sons of former slaves and the sons of former slave owners will be able to sit down together at the table of brotherhood.*
>
> *I have a dream that one day even the state of Mississippi, a state sweltering with the heat of injustice, sweltering with the heat of oppression, will be transformed into an oasis of freedom and justice.*
>
> *I have a dream that my four little children will one day live in a nation where they will not be judged by the color of their skin but by the content of their character.*

I have a dream today.

I have a dream that one day, down in Alabama, with its vicious racists, with its governor having his lips dripping with the words of interposition and nullification; one day right there in Alabama, little black boys and black girls will be able to join hands with little white boys and white girls as sisters and brothers.

I have a dream today.

What pushed Mr. King to keep striving for civil rights legislation when he was beaten and arrested? What kept him going through all of the pain and suffering he faced? His dream that his children can grow up in a nation that doesn't judge them by the color of their skin. His dream that all Americans can join hands. These kept him going when a less convicted man would have quit. His "why" was more powerful than the pain, and that is why he was ultimately successful on his mission.

Without a clearly defined why, you will quit whenever anything becomes difficult because there is no intrinsic motivation to keep going.

So, how do you figure out your why? While I could write an entire book on discovering your why, I have found that clearly defining your goals, values, and purpose is the only way to uncovering your why for your business.

> **IMPORTANT**
>
> Follow the exercises in this chapter both for your personal life and your business. It important that you keep the two separate, but complete the activities for both aspect of your life.

Follow this four step process and uncover your why, which can be anything from being a good example for your son to saving our species. It is your why. It is your internal motivation. Let it be authentic to you.

FIRST STEP – THE WHAT

When I was 21 years old, I made a goal to become a millionaire by the time I was 25. I promised that I would commit everything to this goal, and I did. I went all in. For four years I grinded to hit this goal. Lo and behold, by the time I was 25 . . . I still was not a millionaire. Not even close.

Why did I open up the section on goal setting by telling you about a time I missed a major goal in my life?

Two Reasons:

 To show you that everyone misses goals. Do not let the anxiety or fear of missing goals stop you from setting big ones. Leave that for the average people.

2 To show you that the most important part about goal setting is not actually in hitting the goal, it is who you become while on the adventure to hit the goal. I was not a millionaire at twenty five, but I was a completely different person than I was at twenty one because of trying to hit that goal. Goal setting has completely changed my life

Before you know why you want what you want, it is helpful to determine what you actually want.

First, you need to create a few goals. A dream is just a dream until it is written down. Only then does it become a goal. Break down your goals into 30 day goals, quarterly goals, one year goals, five year goals, ten year goals, and lifetime goals..

When the time comes, get out a pen and paper and actually write down your goals. It's important to see them in front of you. Hang your goals somewhere that you will see them every day. You are far more likely to hit your goals if you are constantly held accountable. After all, a goal is a promise to yourself.

David Vermeeren (international speaker and bestselling author on goal setting and human performance) states that most people claim to understand the importance of goal setting in order to attain a better life, but, in fact, approximately 80 percent of people never set goals for themselves.

Eighty percent of the world does not set goals! Shocking! Warning: most people think all goals are one time goals that you cross off at completion. While bucket list goals such as skydiving could fall under that category, setting a goal is really about changing yourself for the long-term. Vermeeren adds, "Goals aren't short-term, quick-fix things; they are fixed and immovable destinations that show the world who you want to become or what you want to achieve."

This book is not just another book to pummel through before you go on to the next one in your list. Really use these steps to help you.

QUICK TIPS ON GOAL SETTING:

1. Goals can change. As you grow or discover yourself more, your goals will change. Goals should only change, though, because your why or mind set changes. Changing a goal because it is too hard is quitting.

2. Always ask yourself, "Why am I setting this goal. Does this need to be my goal." Challenge the validity or relevance of your goals.

3. Tactical goals should be quantifiable beyond argument. For life goals, you should be able to say deep down whether you hit them or not. Helpful hint: always attach a number to your tactical goals.

You cannot hit a goal, until you become a person that is capable of hitting that goal.

The most important part about goals is the journey they take you on. It's who you become while on the journey that matters. It's where life takes you when you're going for your dreams that you'll remember forever

SECOND STEP – THE HOW

Distinguish your values in life. As a business owner, it is important to do this on a personal level first, then complete the exercise for your company.

The best way to do this is to ask yourself, "What do I want people to say at my funeral?"

Imagine that 60 years from now, you are dead and all of your friends and family are at your funeral. What will they say about you? What do you want them to say about you?

When doing this, close your eyes and think about that question. Write down all your thoughts on a piece of paper. Whatever comes to your mind, write it down. This is a free-write exercise, so phrases, sentences, and words are all fine to write down.

Realize that what you want people to say is what you value most in life. This will be the set of values that you must use as you pursue all of your goals and missions.

> *You can never achieve a worthy end with unworthy means.*

The things you want people to say about you at your funeral are the values you must live by. If you want someone to say you were reliable, then you have to be reliable. It's that easy.

As you continue on your journey of life, if you keep these values in mind, you will get far more fulfillment than you ever imagined possible.

For your business, come up with 3-6 values that are authentic to your company. These should be values that you already embody. They should not be optimistic or values to strive for. The values should represent what is actually important to your company and how you will benchmark every potential employee.

For example at my company, The Limitless Entrepreneur (losethelimits.com), our values are:

Ownership: Own your work, own your mistakes

Integrity: Do what's right, not what's easy

Impact: Exponential Impact

Team: Only hire the best people

Growth: Always improving

THIRD STEP – MAJOR PURPOSE

Now that you have your goals (what you want) and values (how you want to achieve these things), it is time to create your own major purpose. Think of this as your major "what." Think big and figure out what your mission in life is. What were you put here to do? How do you get fulfillment? What do you want to accomplish? What purpose will drive you?

This major "what" can be broad or specific.

My purpose is to be an example for people and prove that you can really have it all, fulfillment, freedom, and love, no matter what circumstance. To inspire and give people the tools to go after what truly makes them happy in life.

Your major purpose can be about experiences, lessons, helping others, whatever you want it to be. Don't get stressed out when it comes to putting the pen to paper regarding a major purpose. It does not have to be perfect. Do not let the thought, "If I don't get it right now, I'll never get it" stop you from creating a major purpose. That is a prime example of a limiting belief.

Don't try to make an eloquent mission statement, which usually comes out cliche and stale, when creating a purpose for your business. The purpose for your business should be authentic to you as the owner and the company as a whole.

Think like Facebook. Their purpose, or mission, is to "Give people the power to build community and bring the world closer together." It's authentic, it's simple, it's real.

Your purpose can change as time goes on. You grow, you evolve. It is natural that your purpose and whys do too. Find your major purpose and write it down. Keep it next to your goals.

FOURTH STEP –THE WHY

Why do you do what you do? Why are your goals your goals? Why is that your purpose? Why do you even want to grow your company?

It is now time to reflect on your goals, values, and purpose to come up with why you have these. Where have these feelings spawned from? Every time you come up with an answer, ask "why" again until you get to the root of the problem. Once you feel that you are at the core of your values and goals, you are at your why.

Figuring out your why can be very difficult alone, so I suggest talking with others about these questions. Your why may also take a few sessions of asking these questions and may stir up some uncomfortable feelings. That means you are getting close. Discovering your why is a vital step to self-discovery. Keep working at it until you have something that resonates and motivates you.

THE WHAT, THE HOW, THE WHY

Now you have the tools necessary to discover your goals, values, purpose, and your why. But how does that help you break your limiting beliefs and help you create the business you want?

It doesn't, by itself. If you simply view them as words on paper, then that is all they are. You must frequently refer back to them – use them as a weapon against your limiting beliefs. Use them to motivate you when times get tough. When you feel like quitting, reflect on these core tools. When you are making a decision, it can be anything, you must think about your values and goals. Ask yourself, "Will this decision ultimately get me to my why and goals?" Then ask yourself, "This decision may get me to my goal, but am I upholding my values by doing it?" Constantly referring back to your why, purpose, and values and then making decisions with them in mind, will keep you on track to achieve success.

REAL TALK

Tony Robbins created a non-profit called the Basket Brigade which delivers baskets of food to impoverished families on Thanksgiving and Christmas. Their purpose is to feed one billion families, which they are well on their way to doing. This is a fantastic purpose and I am sure it drives Tony and his employees. What is more meaningful, though, is why he wants to feed one billion families.

When Tony was eleven years old, his family didn't have enough money to afford a Thanksgiving dinner. They were poor and barely got by. On Thanksgiving Day, his parents were bitterly fighting, spewing hatred at each other while Tony tried to shield his younger brother and sister from hearing the fight. All of sudden there came a knock at the door. Tony, being the oldest, answered the door to find a tall man holding a huge basket of food and an uncooked turkey. Although his father tried to refuse the gift, the stranger insisted they take the food.

This stranger saved Thanksgiving for Tony's family and made him realize that strangers care. And if strangers care about him, Tony would care about strangers. At seventeen, Tony repaid the kindness and delivered two baskets of food to two impoverished families. The next year he delivered food to four families. From there the mission grew into the Basket Brigade.

The road to today was not easy for Tony Robbins. He struggled just as everyone else does. But he didn't let those obstacles get in the way of his purpose. He used his "why" to motivate and drive him. This purpose, combined with Tony's why, has led him on the journey to where he is today, helping millions of people through his books, events, and non-profits.

Remember the Robert Frost quote of two roads diverging in a wood. People without a why and a mind full of limiting beliefs take the road more traveled 10 out of 10 times. Be different.

Put your why on your wall in your bedroom so you have to see it every day. Even if it's personal. Being proud of your why is the best way to hold yourself accountable. Don't be closed off to people knowing your why. It makes you vulnerable which gives you strength. Tell people about your purpose. You will receive more support than you could ever imagine.

CHAPTER RECAP:

1. The most important principle to breaking limiting beliefs and building the life and business you want is having a clear why and a major purpose.

2. Writing goals on paper and putting them on your wall makes you more likely to accomplish your goals.

3. Ask yourself, "What do I want people to say at my funeral?" Write down the answers to find what you value most in life.

4. While finding your why can be tough, creating/finding a life purpose is a great way to get started.

5. Your why, mission, values, and goals are just words on paper if you do not embody them. Look at all decisions, small or large, and decide which option brings you closer to these goals while upholding your values.

6. Put your why on the wall. Do not be afraid to share your why, it will actually make people respect you more. Don't underestimate the power of vulnerability.

7. It is important to create a why, values, purpose, and goals for your company after you have done it on a personal level.

8. Don't forget to complete the steps and activities in this chapter for both your business and your personal life. Keep them separate!

A LOOK AHEAD:

In the next chapter, I will share with you the secret that dozens of millionaires have used to get to where they are. It is what will separate you from the average business owner!!

CHAPTER TOOLS

Life Goals: ....
....

....

....

....

10 Year Goals: ....

....

....

....

....

5 Year Goals: ....

....

....

....

....

1 Year Goals: ....

....

....

....

....

Current Quarter Goals: ....

....

....

....

....

1 Month Goals: ....

....

....

....

....

VALUES

"What do you want the closest people in your life to say about you at your funeral?" (This is a 5 minute free write. Write whatever words, sentences, or phrases come to mind.)

....

....

....

....

....

....

....

....

....

PURPOSE

What is your major purpose?

WHY

What is your why? ....

....

....

....

....

BUSINESS ACTIVITIES

What is the one year goal for your business (go to the end of the current calendar year)

....

....

....

....

....

....

Quarterly goals? ....

....

....

....

....

....

....

This month's goals?

What are your company's 3-6 core values? This works really well as an exercise with all partners and may take some time.

What is your company's purpose?

Why did you start or why do you want to start your company?

....

....

....

....

....

....

....

....

....

....

....

....

....

....

KEY 2: FAILURE

"

I've missed more than 9000 shots in my career.
I've lost almost 300 games. Twenty-six times, I've
been trusted to take the game-winning shot and
missed. I've failed over and over and over again in
my life. And that is why I succeed.
– MICHAEL JORDAN

Failure. The two syllable word that ruins so many people's lives. Failure renders you useless, intimidated, and frozen. That is at least what you think.

Failure doesn't actually do any of that. It is the fear of failure that ruins lives and renders you frozen in your unfulfilled world. The fear of failure has stopped many more business ventures than actual failure ever has. We, as humans, are so afraid of failing that we'd rather just not go for it.

You would rather never obtain "it" than face the risk of embarrassment, of "failure."

You stay on your shores of comfort so that you dare not tempt fate and risk failing at anything. You keep your business at a level you have outgrown rather than go to the next level and risk looking bad. You let opportunities pass you by so that you're not disappointed if it doesn't work out. You don't pursue that dream you've always had.

You eventually let life pass you by all so that you can avoid this scary term called "failure."

Life doesn't have to be that way though. The truly successful people have figured this out. There is another way.

The next key to breaking limiting beliefs and achieving ultimate business success is to know you cannot fail. Someone with limiting beliefs may write this principle off and tell me that you can definitely fail. Let me tell my story of the first time I heard this principle in use.

REAL TALK

I first heard this principle from a man named Chris Coutinho, and the conversation we had about this topic *completely changed my life*. I had the great fortune to let Chris know a year later how deeply he had impacted me.

Chris runs a seven figure logistics company and lives the lifestyle he wants. He and his wife have been married for over 20 years; he spends time with his kids every day and has a great relationship with them. He does most of his office work on a boat in the middle of the lake he and his family live on. He is literally living his version of the dream.

I met Chris by winning a competition set up by the company I worked for in college. By being one of the top two sales leaders in my division, I earned a day out on Chris' boat with him and other millionaires who used to work at the same company.

During the same time that I earned this boat trip, I was really struggling with my business. I was in a negative state of mind because I recently had to let go of all of my employees and start from scratch. Being with all of these wildly successful people only made me feel worse because I thought to myself, "I could never be this successful, I have already failed at running my first business."

Chris noticed my state of depression. He took me aside and started to tell me about his life and all of his struggles before he made his millions and had the life he always dreamed of. He made a million, lost a million, then made it all back again.

The conversation helped, but it did not really resonate with me. I kept thinking, "Yeah, but that is you, not me." All of a sudden, he said something that has stuck with me and guided me ever since. He looked me right in the eyes and said, "It's great because you don't even know how successful you are going to be." I asked him what he meant, to which he replied, "Because you can't fail."

I replied, "Yeah, yeah. You can't fail. Positivity like that is important. It is a good mentality to have."

He shot back, "No, you don't understand. You literally can't fail." I thought at this time he may have had a couple too many drinks.

"If you just keep going in life, you can't fail. No matter what. Every time something bad happens, it's not failure. As Napoleon Hill says, 'Most great people have attained their greatest success just one step beyond their greatest failure.' The only failure in life is if you quit, and I know you're not a quitter," said Chris.

Those simple words changed my whole mentality about business, competition, and, most importantly, life. "As long as you keep going in life, you can't fail."

He was right. You can't fail. Losing all of my employees was not failing, failing would have been to quit. It was an opportunity to challenge my problem solving skills. That weekend I went home and hired a whole new team. By the end of the summer, I wound up winning the Performance Under Pressure award in my company.

SUZUKI

The Suzuki name was made famous by Michio Suzuki who founded his company in 1909. While Suzuki is a world famous automotive brand today, it wasn't always a car manufacturer. Michio actually began by manufacturing weaving looms for Japan's giant silk industry. He built his loom company for the next thirty years with modest success.

Michio knew that diversifying his company would benefit it greatly. In 1937 he decided to start manufacturing automobiles. He spent two years developing prototype cars and building a facility. He was ready to start producing his cars when Japan took over his factories to assist with the World War II effort.

His plans were halted completely. During the war his factory was bombed and destroyed. He spent months and millions of dollars rebuilding his factory in hopes that he would eventually be able to manufacture automobiles. When he finally finished rebuilding his factory, it was bombed and destroyed again. Luckily, after the war, domestic textile manufacturing orders started to soar and his loom company rode the wave. He was finally able to rebuild his factory.

This success was short lived, however, as the cotton market crashed in 1951, desiccating his loom company. He now needed to rebuild his loom company while simultaneously re-starting his automotive plans. He did not have the capacity to start mass producing cars right away so he started to make motorized bicycles.

This was an instant hit and saved his companies from crashing. Since then the company has scaled to become one of the largest car manufacturers in the world. Michio's legacy lives on through his company, which is still run by his family.

It is because of Michio's endurance that the world knows the name Suzuki. It is because Michio would not quit that his company became one of the largest in its industry. Michio could have deemed himself a failure many times during his journey. He knew, though, that as long as he didn't quit, he couldn't fail.

FEAR SETTING: AN EXERCISE ON ACCEPTING FAILURE

A way to bring about this belief that you cannot fail is to do an ancient stoic exercise called "Fear Setting" that has been made famous by Tim Ferris. This will help you accept the concept that you cannot fail as long as you are always moving forward.

In the exercise, examine a decision you are thinking about. For example, maybe you want to start a new division of your company. That is definitely scary. First, you look at the worst case scenarios of making this decision.

You then analyze each worst case scenario and think of ways to prevent the scenario from happening. Using the same scenario, you then assume that scenario happened and ask yourself how you would repair the situation. You then rate each worst case scenario based on how life altering and permanent these would be.

After you go through the worst case scenario exercise, write down what the benefits of a partial success or attempt look like.

Finally, factor in the cost of inaction. If you stay in the same position, how would your life look one year from now? Five years from now?

After all of this data and thinking, the decision will be very clear. Fear setting is a great way to challenge your fears, especially your fears around failure.

> NOTE
> There is a section to do your own fear setting
> exercise at the end of this chapter.

It is important to avoid fighting the acceptance of this key, failure. When you avoid the acceptance of failure, you really have the limiting belief that you lack the necessary confidence needed to avoid failure. Let me remind you that it is not about the concept of confidence at all, but it is the knowledge of knowing that you cannot fail.

It is not an opinion, it is a fact. Once you agree to that fact, the confidence will come from that. This concept goes against everything society tells you your whole life, so you do have to be a little crazy to accept it. But once you do, you will join the list of wildly successful people who also know and adhere to this fact of life.

Some examples of other successful people using this principle include:

ROBERT KIYOSAKI – Author of the #1 personal finance book of all time – *Rich Dad, Poor Dad* – and millionaire entrepreneur
He states in his book, "Most people are not rich because they are terrified of losing. Winners are not afraid of losing. But losers are. Failure is part of the process of success. People who avoid failure also avoid success."

DWAYNE "THE ROCK" JOHNSON – Highest grossing actor of 2014 & 2016
One The Rock's most famous quotes reads, "In 1995, I had $7 bucks in my pocket and knew two things: I'm broke as hell and one day I won't be."

MARK CUBAN – Owner of the Dallas Mavericks and billionaire entrepreneur
Mark Cuban used to sleep on the floor of a three bedroom apartment with five other roommates. He knew that he was going to be wildly successful someday. "Because if you're prepared and you know what it takes, it's not a risk. You just have to figure out how to get there. There is always a way to get there."

THOMAS EDISON - Inventor of the electric light
Edison failed 10,000 times before he invented the electric light. To which he said, "I have not failed. I've just found 10,000 ways that won't work."

COLONEL SANDERS - Founder of KFC

Sanders was turned down over 1,000 times before he found a buyer for his chicken recipe.

DR. SEUSS - American Pulitzer prize winning writer and cartoonist famous for his children's books

Dr. Seuss' first children's book was rejected by 27 publishers before the 28th publisher sold six million copies.

CHAPTER RECAP:

① The second key to breaking your limiting beliefs is: Know that you cannot fail.

② This concept is not about having a confident mindset, but accepting this statement as a fact.

③ The most successful people in the world know how to use this principle to live the life they want.

④ Fear setting is an exercise used by the ancient stoics to reduce your fear of failure and gain clarity on tough decisions.

Every adversity, every failure,
every heartache carries with it the seed
of an equal or greater benefit.
-NAPOLEON HILL

A LOOK AHEAD:

You will look at what really separates the people who get what they want in life and the people who don't. The next key challenges you to look at every decision you make while creating a system for success.

CHAPTER TOOLS

What are you afraid to fail at?

What does that "failure" look like?

Is there a lesson to be learned from that outcome?
Is it really failure?

FEAR SETTING

What if I ....

.... ?

What are the worst case scenarios?

1. ....

....

2. ....

....

3. ....

....

How can you prevent each one?

1. ....

....

2. ....

....

3. ....

....

How can you repair the situation if they happen?

1. ....

....

2. ....

....

3. ....

....

What are the benefits of a success or a partial success?

....

....

....

....

....

....

....

What is the cost of inaction?

1 Year from now? ....

....

....

....

....

....

....

5 Years from now? ....

....

....

....

....

....

....

KEY 3: HABIT

"

We are what we repeatedly do.
Excellence, therefore, is not an act, but a habit.
- ARISTOTLE

Do the Thing and You Will Have the Power

Peyton Manning is known as one of the best NFL quarter-backs of all time. "The Sheriff," as many people call him, exposed weaknesses in any defense he played against. He would command the field, knowing the perfect play to call just by seeing where the defenders were lined up.

It was truly amazing to watch. So, what was the source of his almost magical ability to spot these weaknesses and call the perfect play at the perfect time? It was his habits.

From his college days to his last year in the NFL, Manning's teammates have always praised his study habits. It is said that Peyton Manning studied his playbooks and films more than any other NFL player. Manning would often call new wide receivers to his hotel room at 9:45 p.m. at night after a long day of training camp to run extra drills with them for twenty minutes. When older quarterbacks are taking their last few years easy, Peyton pushed even harder, studying more and learning more.

What makes Peyton truly special is that he not only has great habits and study skills, he also loves the process. He's learned to love the behind the scenes work that leads to success.

Denver offensive coordinator, Adam Gase, says Manning always enjoyed what could be considered the mundane aspects of being a quarterback: studying, installing, practicing, playing in preseason games and working out. "He is eating up every minute of this," claimed Gase.

Kobe Bryant, one of the greatest basketball players of all time, was known for his intense work ethic. He would frequently be at the training facility running conditioning drills and shooting around at 4:00am .

Mark Zuckerberg, Founder of Facebook, commits to reading a book every two weeks.

A quick look at individuals with sustained, long term success shows that they don't just show up and are immediately great. They work hard for it. They create the habits in their life that result in this long term success.

Your habits make you who you are. Habits can lift us to a full life, or they can drag us down to an unfulfilled and ultimately unhappy life. Our habits literally make or break our success in our personal and business life.

Good thing we can control our habits.

In order to break your limiting beliefs, you need to constantly create habits that support your why. If one of your goals is to run a marathon, you need to get into the habit of training every day. One day skipped and it could ruin your entire training regimen.

To get anything in life, you must create excellent habits. You are always moving either toward your goals, or away from them. Positive habits move you closer to your goals. Negative habits move you in the opposite direction.

Negative habits pull you away from your goals and perpetuate your limiting beliefs. Not all negative habits are obvious, though. A negative habit could also have a neutral effect on your life. If a habit you have is not getting you closer to your goals, it is negative. It is as simple as that.

REAL TALK

Examining habits from that same lens, binge watching Netflix is a common negative habit these days. It doesn't necessarily have a directly negative impact on life, but it is in no way getting you closer to your goals. In fact, it wastes valuable time that you can use to be as successful as you can be or simply spend more quality time with the people you love.

But you can work to mitigate this negative habit. If this is your negative habit, you can't just go cold turkey and stop watching all shows. So make a rule. Don't start new shows until the one you're currently watching ends. Just by creating this small "rule," you slowly reduce your time of watching television until you finally have it down to maybe two to three hours a week.

You will be much more productive with your days if you follow this rule, which will attribute to your success. Besides the productivity boost, it will also force you to use your "down time" in more proactive and ultimately more fulfilling ways.

THE FIXED MINDSET VS. THE GROWTH MINDSET

If knowing your "why" is what gets you to start pursuing your dreams and business ventures, creating positive habits is what keeps you in pursuit.

Creating positive habits is one of the hardest keys to follow because, just like limiting beliefs, your habits become a part of your life. You make an agreement with yourself that the habits you have cannot be controlled. It is just who you are. With that "agreement" comes helplessness. Comes despair. You feel enslaved by your habits.

This creates what Carol Dweck calls a fixed mindset. Having a fixed mindset means you believe that things in life are immovable, unchangeable. A person with the fixed mindset believes that they are born the way they are and they can't change it. This is where the feeling of helplessness stems from. How can someone feel empowered if they think they can't change the way they are? Having this fixed mindset can ruin their life. It prevents them from seeking change, from trying new things. This prevents the business owner from reinventing his business or working on a weakness that will greatly improve his business. This can lead to depression and anxiety, hopelessness.

Many people go their entire lives living with this self-sustaining Hell they have put themselves in; using their fixed mindset to think they're not good enough, and never will be because they can't change. This results in worse and worse habits which only strengthens these fixed mindsets. It is a vicious cycle-- a terrible feedback loop.

On the other hand, there are others who feel *empowered* by their mindset. They know they can change things in their life. That the cure to not being smart enough is to study harder or get better mentors. These people do not allow circumstance to dictate their life.

These people have what is known as the growth mindset. If the fixed mindset is what strengthens limiting beliefs and negative habits, the growth mindset is what destroys limiting beliefs and allows a person to create positive habits.

Being aware of when you have a fixed mindset and a growth mindset is one of the most important aspects to creating and maintaining positive habits.

Habits have a drastic impact on your life. To realize the impact of positive habits, you need to start implementing them into your daily life. Here are the leading habits for moving the needle in your business:

EXERCISE

One of the most crucial habits you can implement into your life is exercise. Use your workouts to cleanse your body and mind. This allows you to push your body while keeping yourself present.

Working out consistently also has a huge impact on your business. Exercise primes you for the work day, both mentally and physically. Creating a daily habit around exercise also gives your day structure. The workouts keep you grounded. Jocko Willink, former U.S. Navy Seal Team Leader and leadership consultant to fortune 500 companies, sums up why exercise is important perfectly, ""It's about hard work. It's about consistency. It's about getting up in the morning and getting it done." He also preaches that, "Discipline equals freedom." By having a preset schedule for working out each morning, you are saving yourself from decision fatigue and giving yourself more freedom to execute at a higher level.

THE MORNING ROUTINE

Another crucial positive habit is having a concrete morning routine. Tony Robbins and Tim Ferris say their morning routines were a major reason for their success today. Many other icons have said the same thing about their morning routines. Starting the day off with a positive habit is the BEST way to start your day.

My morning routine has changed numerous times over the past few years as I have tried different things. I ultimately landed on the few tasks that work for me. Everyone is different (Tony Robbins prefers a cold plunge first thing in the morning) so I'd suggest trying different activities until you settle on what works for you.

Morning routine suggestion:

- **Making a superfood shake** and warming up pre made steel cut oatmeal. You don't want to waste time in the morning so this is a fast way to get breakfast made and move on to other items.
- **Journaling** three things you are grateful for (one person, one opportunity, and one small item). Then free write whatever is on your mind for a few paragraphs. This allows you to get thoughts on paper without having to put too much pressure on what you are going to write. This makes it a lot more enjoyable.
- **Priming your state**, which is anything that gets you in state. This could be putting on peaceful music (Piano melodies or classical) and taking a few deep breathes or listening to motivational videos and doing some pushups.

- **Reviewing your why, purpose, values, and goals**
- **Visualizing or meditating** for 10 minutes. When you visualize, think about what your perfect future life looks like. Then work backwards to what you have to do today to get to that perfect life.

This routine should take about forty five minutes and it is safe to say that it is the most important forty five minutes of the day. It primes your state of my mind and gets you ready for anything you will face that day.

The people who make the effort to create this personal time take back control of their life. They begin the day on their terms and focus on themselves. This results in them creating better habits in all areas of their life and breaking their limiting beliefs.

THE HARD STOP

On top of a morning routine, you also need a **hard stop on work at night**. This means that no matter what you are doing, do not do any work past 7:00 p.m. or a time that works best for you. Even if you are in the zone. This forces you to prioritize better during the day and allows you to reenergize for the next day.

The concept for The Hard Stop stems from a story called the "Twenty Mile March."

The "Twenty Mile March" tells the tale of two ships who were racing to discover Antarctica first. Both ships began at the same time from Europe and were well equipped by the monarchs of their respective nations. But their captains had two very different strategies for the race.

The first captain had his ship sail extremely hard every day there was good weather and winds, and proceed slowly on days with bad weather and winds. Some days they would sail eighty miles, some they would sail just five.

The second captain had his ship sail just twenty miles each day, no matter the weather. Even when his crew moaned that they had great winds and the other ship was gaining a lead, he kept to his strategy. Twenty miles a day, no matter what.

Who do you think won the race?

Not only did the second ship that marched twenty miles a day make it there first, but the first ship never made it at all. Every crew member, including the captain died of sickness and fatigue.

Mark Zuckerberg has publicly stated that he works fifty hours a week at Facebook.

John D. Rockefeller, who was arguably the greatest businessman of all time, made it a point to not overwork. He claimed that if his body was drained, then he could not give his all to his work, and that would be a disservice to his company.

It is vitally important to not burn out, your business and personal life depend on you to be at your best.

READ, READ, READ

Another habit that many successful people implement in their life is the habit of reading.

Warren Buffett said that he spends most of his day reading. Mark Zuckerberg reads one book every two weeks in an effort to learn new cultures and ideas. Mark Cuban reads three hours every day. The average CEO reads sixty books a year. When asked what his alma mater was, Malcom X replied, "Books."

This is no coincidence. There is a clear correlation with success, fulfilment, and reading books. When I learned about this, I was not happy. I hated reading books and am generally an extremely slow reader. I never read the assigned reading in school so how could I possibly get to the levels of Mark Zuckerberg and other successful CEOs?

If you are like me, here's what to do: Make it simple. At first, commit to reading for ten minutes per day. No matter what, you should have at least ten minutes every day to read.

Then turn ten minutes into fifteen pages per day (which is 5,475 pages a year). After slowly increasing your page count, you will be reading three or four books each month and love it. Remember, you have the power to create positive habits in your life.

INTEGRITY

Don Miguel Ruiz preaches the importance of habits in his classic, *The Four Agreements*. In the book, Ruiz speaks about four agreements (or habits) that can have an amazing impact in your life if you adopt them.

I am a firm believer in following all of these agreements, but the one that has had the biggest impact in my life is being impeccable to your word.

When you say you are going to do something, do it. This makes you a more reliable person in all of your relationships (personal and business) and makes you more aware of promises you have made to people.

This habit will eventually become a shortcut for decision making. You will no longer have to decide whether you are going to do things or not. If you say you are going to do something, you have to do it.

This habit will also make you a lot more open with your feelings and emotions. You won't say things you don't mean because you are forced to be completely honest, with yourself and others.

While adhering to this habit is a constant struggle, it alone could have the most drastic impact in your life. When you choose to do something with integrity, you are still doing what you want. However, by adopting this habit, you will feel empowered by your decisions, not restricted.

THE LAW OF ATTRACTION

"

The only reason why people do not have what they want is because they are thinking more about what they don't want than what they do want. Listen to your thoughts, and listen to the words you are saying. The law is absolute and there are no mistakes.

- THE SECRET, BY RHONDA BYRNE

Your focus becomes your reality. On the surface, the quote by Rhonda Byrne may seem a bit mystical or "woo-woo." Most people (usually the unhappy or unfulfilled ones) will say that reality is reality, and your focus has nothing to do with it. However, the Law of Attraction and all of the concept's famous followers will strongly disagree.

The law of attraction is the belief that by focusing on positive or negative thoughts, a person brings positive or negative experiences into their life. Quite literally, your focus becomes your reality.

Have you ever noticed that the person who is always complaining and crying victim is always having negative experiences? It is almost as if they are a magnet to negative events. That is because they are. By focusing on the negative they are attracting only negative. By always seeing themselves as a victim, they are creating a world in which they are always the victim.

You see this in everyday life. You go out into the big world in search of negativity. You focus on the bad weather, how much you hate your current role, or on that parking ticket you received.

You focus on how helpless and stuck you are, which then makes you feel helpless and stuck, which then makes you act helpless and stuck. It is a vicious cycle that builds a habit over time, the habit of focusing on the negative.

You not only focus on the negative, you visualize the negative. You tell yourself you are going to be late. You imagine getting cheated on. You visualize performing badly at your investor meeting. You envision negative events, which then make your body feel as if these events are happening already. This puts you in a negative mindset which leads us to what? That's right, more negativity.

As humans, we are so used to focusing on the negative that we have made it a social norm. How many friends do you talk about dreams, goals, and your positive futures with? Not many I bet. How many "friends" do you complain about work to? Or gossip about how much you do not like a person? Or brag about how lazy you were this weekend?

With all of this social conditioning, it is extremely hard to break the mold and use the Law of Attraction to your benefit. But just because it is hard doesn't mean you can't do it.

You must do it. It is imperative to your life and your business. Your focus becomes your reality.

We all have the choice, in every situation, to focus on what we want to. By being vigilant, you can create the habit of visualizing success. You can create the habit of being positive. You can stay grateful for every experience. You can use the Law of Attraction to become a happier, more fulfilled person.

Create your reality. Just focus on the positive.

THE FILTER

There I was, staring at the mountains in Park City, Utah. My business was struggling to get going, I had to borrow money to pay my mortgage, I just got out of a serious relationship, and to top it off I was making bad personal decisions (skipping workouts, partying too often, etc.). It was one of the lowest points of my life. I felt like my life was tail spinning out of control. I felt helpless.

In the midst of all of this turmoil, I went on a trip to Sundance Film Festival with my mother for her birthday (luckily I paid for this trip well before I started the business). It was there in Utah that I would have some of the most impactful few days of my entire life.

Being away from my day to day, and being in such a beautiful place, I was able to take a step back and examine what exactly was going on with my life. I looked at the big picture. Where did I go wrong? What was causing my issues? Where did these problems stem from? I dwelled on these questions for a few days, until suddenly, while taking in the beauty of the snow covered mountain ranges, I realized the answer:

It was me.

Or more accurately, it was my decisions and actions. I had all of these ideas for what I wanted in my life, both in the present and in the future, but my actions did not align with these goals.

Was partying getting me closer to my goals? No.
Was sleeping in getting me closer to my goals? No.
Was skipping workouts getting me closer to my goals? No.
Was drinking liquor getting me closer to my goals? No.

I felt empowered. I knew right there that I had the power to turn things around. I committed to myself right there in Park City that for every decision I had to make going forward, I would ask myself, "**Is doing this going to get me closer to the life I want?**" If that answer was no, then I would not do it. If that answer was yes, then I would do it no matter what. This instantly made tough decisions easier.

I immediately stopped partying, which led to a much more fulfilled life. I started waking up at 5:30am to exercise before work. I committed to my morning routine, no matter how tired I was. I cut out liquor completely from my life. I started focusing on the positives and using the Law of Attraction in my favor. I became vigilant about my thoughts, constantly reframing situations to make them positive.

I began to run each decision I made through "The Filter" of getting me closer to the life I want to live.

The results were instantaneous. My business started to grow rapidly. I started to become healthier and more fulfilled. As a result I was happier.

Applying The Filter drastically improved my life and continues to guide me on the right path today. It helps me implement the habits I need to achieve the life I want and take my business in the direction I want it to go.

The best way to build positive habits and rid yourself of negative habits is to look at every decision you make through "The Filter". Ask yourself this question: **"Is this decision getting me closer to my ultimate goals in life?"** If it doesn't, it is not worth doing.

If you really want to write a book or be healthier in life, would going out with your friends four nights a week get you closer to the goals? Absolutely not, so why do most people wind up making these decisions? Because they don't look at their decisions through the filter. They then get into the habit of making bad decisions.

You probably have a habit of making bad decisions and don't even notice it. If you look through the filter and reflect on every decision you make, you will see yourself starting to break that negative habit of making bad decisions. You will then start to create a new positive habit of making positive decisions. If you can manage to get into the habit of making positive decisions, it will then become second nature.

Think of a life lived without any regrets. Isn't that what we all want? Strive to live a life where you feel positive about every decision you make.

CHALLENGE

Examine all of the decisions you make in a week. Use the filter to ask yourself if your actions are getting you closer to your ultimate goals. Write these decisions down in a journal and after the week, look back to see the results. What can you change? What decisions clearly did not get you closer to your goals? Begin to create the habit of using The Filter to guide your actions.

"

Success isn't always about 'Greatness.'
It's about consistency. Consistent hard work
gains success. Greatness will come

— THE ROCK

The above quote embodies the power of habit. Greatness isn't this magical thing inside certain people. Greatness comes to those who consistently put in the time to be great. It is a habit, not an act.

Ask yourself, how many positive habits do you have in your life? How many negative habits do you have? Create an action plan to get rid of these negative habits and you will see an instant improvement.

CHAPTER RECAP:

1. The principle of developing positive habits is one of the third key for breaking limiting beliefs and creating the life/business you want.

2. Positive habits add value to your life and get you closer to your life goals.

3   Negative habits are any habits that do not get you closer to the life you want to live. They either take you further from your goals or they do not bring you any closer.

4   A morning routine is used by successful people all over the globe to start their day off right.

5   Having a hard stop to work keeps you refreshed.

6   Reading just ten pages a day will help you learn the skills necessary to rapidly grow your business.

7   When you are making decisions in your life, you must ask yourself, "Is this decision getting me closer to my ultimate goals?" Using this filter will instantly reveal whether a habit is positive or negative.

8   Excellence and greatness are not acts, but habits. Remember, we are what we repeatedly do.

EXTRA TOOL

Check out www.losethelimits.com/habitbuilder-calendar to download your free habit builder calendar. This is what I use to implement positive habits in my own life.

LOOK AHEAD:

The next key is "People." This key is critical to overcoming limiting beliefs and having a successful business. It is one of the harder keys to adopt, but also the one that shows results the quickest.

CHAPTER TOOLS

1. Write down 3 positive habits you already have established in your life: ....

....

....

....

2. Write down 3 negative habits you have in your life:

....

....

....

....

3. Write down 3 specific situations you have focused on the negatives? Was there any positive that was overlooked?

....

....

....

....

....

....

....

....

....

....

....

....

....

....

4. In what areas of your life do you possess the Growth Mindset? (Physical, wealth, health, mental.)

....

....

....

....

....

....

5. In what areas of your life do you possess the Fixed Mindset?

....

....

....

....

6. Potential Morning Routine

Use the lines below to outline what your morning routine will look like.

KEY 4: PEOPLE

"

Keep away from people who try to belittle your ambitions. Small people always do that. But the really great make you feel that you too can become great.

- MARK TWAIN

You are the average of the five people you spend the most time with.

- JIM ROHN

Have you ever been around someone who you just could not help but feel better around? The type of person who empowered you to believe you could do almost anything in the world?

Growing up where I did, with a lot of negative people, I was extremely lucky to have two parents who never belittled my dreams. They pushed me to be better and reach for my dreams when others around me tried to drag me down. My god-father Bob, who was a second father to me, always told me to live my life to its fullest and chase everything I wanted in life.

He preached about living my life with "no what ifs."

Every time I was around Bob I felt like I could do anything in the world. I was also lucky to find a mentor in high school who would do this to an even larger level. My high school wrestling coach, who I looked up to almost as much as my parents and Bob, guided me and told me I was capable of great things. When I failed or was close to quitting, he would pull me back up (metaphorically and a lot of times physically) and refuse to let me quit. Whenever there was a tough time in my life, he was there to listen.

I didn't realize it at the time, but these people were pivotal to my success in life. As Mark Twain mentions, they never belittled my ambitions and always made me feel as though I can become great.

You can either fall into one of two categories: You are either surrounded by people who enable your fixed mindset or people who provide you with a growth environment. If you are surrounded by people with a fixed mindset, this chapter is going to be a tough pill to swallow because you have to make the necessary changes to surround yourself with people who want to succeed in life as bad as you do. This logic is backed by the law of association.

The Law of Association is the concept that like minded people are attracted to one another. **You become the average of the five closest people in your life.** Think about that. If this concept is true, one of the surest ways to break down your limiting beliefs in life and become the successful person you want to become is to simply surround yourself with successful people who do not have limiting beliefs. Who are the five closest people in your life? Can you say for sure that all five of them are making you the person you want to be? Are they bringing you up or pulling you down?

If you associate with negative, belittling people, you will eventually start to think like them. Failures and negative people are like quicksand, they will do whatever it takes to pull you down with them. It is sad and hard to admit, but not all of your friends want to see you be successful. The more you succeed, the more they feel like losers.

Some "Friends" will put down your goals and try to almost sabotage your success. They do not understand why you want it and will attack your way of life, putting your dreams down as "impossible" or "unrealistic." This is what little people do because misery loves company.

But, if you surround yourself with truly great people, you will start to feel that you can be truly great. You will start to think, "If they did it, why not me."

The Law of Association is of the utmost importance to the success of your business. Make it your mission to rid yourself of negative influences and surround yourself with only positive, motivated people. Positivity breeds positivity. Your circle should be made up of all the people you truly admire. They should be people that you look at and say, "I will be like them one day." You should constantly be attempting to learn from and emulate your circle.

LINCOLN'S "TEAM OF RIVALS"

When Abraham Lincoln was elected President of the United States in 1860, he made an unprecedented move that would ultimately help steer the nation through the Civil War. He decided to appoint his three fiercest rivals to his cabinet.

These three rivals were bitter opponents to Lincoln during the primaries and held vastly different views than he. Normal convention of the time said to fill your cabinet with like-minded individuals so you can push your agenda forward. Lincoln knew though that you are the average of the five people closest to you.

His explanation at the time was that these were the strongest men in the country. He declared that at a time of peril, the country needed to have the strongest men, and that he couldn't deprive it of those talents. Lincoln also knew that he too needed these men around him to challenge him and ultimately make him better. He not only filled his cabinet with these three rivals, but he also added to his cabinet a list of men whom he considered all smarter than he.

This cabinet would not only guide the country through its darkest days, it would also help cement Lincoln's legacy as one of the greatest presidents of all time.

These three rivals not only helped Lincoln politically and professionally, but they eventually all became some of Lincoln's closest friends. William H. Seward, who started as Lincoln's biggest rival, ultimately wrote to his wife in a letter, "The President is the best of us."

By understanding the importance of who you have in your circle and who you spend time with, Lincoln made the tough but correct decision and changed the course of history.

To be great, you must keep great company.
Steel sharpens steel.

Surrounding yourself with like minded individuals that challenge you like President Lincoln won't just come now that you are aware of it. You must actively search out great people and make an effort to keep them close to you.

One of the biggest blame shifts regarding this principle is, "Well, I don't know anybody great." Or, "Well, no one great would want to associate with me." Those are both terrible limiting beliefs. There is without a doubt someone great in or near your area – you just have to go find them.

And regarding "I'm not good enough," if you think you are not good enough for someone to talk to, realize that that doesn't matter. Talk to them anyway. That is the point of being around people you look up to. The more you associate with people that are way out of your league, the more you will learn and eventually become like them.

You must shift your circle of influence to become great. If you want to become a millionaire talk to billionaires to get you there faster.

This law of association also goes for who you look up to. Who are your heroes? They are equally important as your friend group. People all over the world grow up idolizing immoral people, and they start to embody what that person believes. A person I knew had so much potential in the world, but they idolized crooks and gangsters. They eventually followed in the footsteps of their idols because they thought that was the way people should be.

We must look up to people who will make us better people. We should imagine ourselves being them in certain situations. When it comes to coaching, my biggest heroes are Chris Powell and Tony Robbins. When it comes to sports, I imagine myself as Muhammad Ali. When it comes to management and sales, I always try to think what Elon Musk and Simon Sinek would do in these situations. I use these heroes to guide my decisions and my morals. Robert Kiyosaki calls this phenomenon the Power of Myth.

CHALLENGE

Find the smartest person you can find and get in. Ask them if you could interview them about their field or position for some research you are doing for a new project. Ask if they can do a quick lunch or coffee and get to know them. Learn from them.

CHAPTER RECAP:

1. The Law of Association is the theory that like people are attracted to one another.

2. You become the average of the five closest people in your life.

3. You must shift your circle of influence to become who you want to be. If you want to become a millionaire, talk to billionaires to get you there faster.

4. Negativity breeds negativity so if you are around negative people, you are more likely to live a negative life full of limiting beliefs. On the flip side, positivity breeds positivity.

5. Steel sharpens steel, so choose to keep people in your life that make you want to be great.

6. Who you look up to is almost as important as who you keep as friends. Choose your heroes carefully.

A LOOK AHEAD:

The last key embodies all of the keys in their entirety. This last key will show you what it takes to sustain the progress made by making the decision to live by the previous four keys.

CHAPTER TOOLS

Who are the five closest people in your life? Label them positive or negative (be honest with yourself) Do these people elevate your thinking or life? ....

....

....

....

....

....

....

What do the 5 closest people (from above) think about your business? Are they supportive? Are they negative? ....

....

....

....

....

....

....

List three people you respect or look up to that you can reach out to for a meeting.

In regards to your business, who are 3 people who you can talk to that would have an immediate impact to your success?

List your next action steps based on your findings to the four exercises above.

KEY 5: GROWTH

"

Thinking is the hardest work there is.
That is why so few people engage in it.

- HENRY FORD

Our levels of success will rarely exceed
our level of personal development. Because
success is something we attract by
who we become.

- JIM ROHN

Andrew Carnegie, one of the most successful businessmen in history, knew the power of checking your ego and continuing to grow.

Carnegie didn't start out as an aristocrat. He did not come from a rich and powerful family. Carnegie's father was a hand-loom weaver while his mother worked two jobs to keep the family from starving. Carnegie started working when he was 13 years old in a cotton mill factory. He worked 12 hours a day, 6 days a week to help support his family. Carnegie was no ordinary factory worker though. He was always working harder than the other boys and quickly became the boss' favorite employee.

On his days off he would borrow books from a local wealthy man and read. This was his source of education. A year later, on the recommendation of his uncle, Carnegie became a telegraph messenger. He continued with his hard working ways, memorizing all of the locations of businesses in Pittsburgh, PA and the faces of important men. He made connections this way and eventually was promoted to operator.

After five years of working for the telegraph company, Carnegie joined the Pennsylvania Railroad Company as a telegraph operator. Carnegie's boss, Thomas Scott, would become one of the most important mentors in Carnegie's life. Scott taught Carnegie about business, management, and investments. Scott liked Carnegie's drive and willingness to learn. They remained close friends until the end.

Slowly but deliberately, Carnegie moved up the business ladder to eventually become the richest man in the world. However, he wasn't born with the skillset to do this. He learned it along the way. Even at the height of his ascent, Carnegie searched out people who were smarter than him so that he may learn from. He was an avid reader his entire life, always looking for more knowledge.

Carnegie did not hit his goals then stopped learning. He didn't let success coerce him with a false sense confidence. He knew that he must keep growing. He knew that knowledge was the ultimate power. He had no ego when it came to learning, and that resulted in him making history.

The last key to breaking limiting beliefs is growth. Mastering this key means constantly learning from everyone and everything. In order to grow as a person and to exponentially grow your business, **you must check your ego at the door and LEARN**. Remember that everyone can teach you something. Even if it is how not to act, it is still a valuable lesson.

Actively search out things you do not know. Personal development is one of the most important ingredients of living a successful life. It has a direct impact on your business success. Hal Elrod, bestselling author and speaker, explains, "If we fail to make time for personal development, we are forced to make time for pain and struggle."

The story of Socrates and the Oracle of Delphi sum up this chapter very well. The Oracle of Delphi had proclaimed Socrates to be the wisest man in Greece because of Socrates' position on how much he knew. Socrates, a lifelong learner, proclaimed **"I know one thing: that I know nothing."** One of the world's greatest philosophers and learners had absolutely no ego when it came to knowledge. He claimed to know nothing, which made him the wisest man in Greece.

Most people are afraid to "show weakness" and appear stupid. Being closed off and not wanting to seem weak is understandable. Showing humility and opening yourself up to learning can be extremely hard. Opening up is a very vulnerable thing to do, which is scary. This can be especially hard for business owners and people wanting to start a business because they don't want to seem stupid in front of employees, investors, and potential critics. For most, it is a big step out of their comfort zone to be vulnerable and accept that you have so much to learn. The only time people learn, though, is when they are out of their comfort zone.

You cannot grow if you are not being challenged.

In Senninger's Learning Zone Model, the comfort zone is important, as it gives us a safe place to return to. However, in order to learn, we need to be in the learning zone, outside the comfort, but not into the panic zone (Senninger, 2000, cited in ThemPra, ca 2008).

Here is a look at **The Learning Zone Model (Senninger, 2000):**

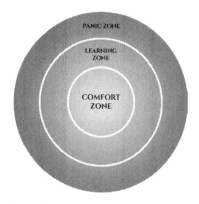

Most people live well within the comfort zone, staying safe. You say no to extra learning. You repeatedly reply "I know" when a person tries to teach you something. You don't ask for help. You don't take on projects that will test you. You choose to stay the big fish in a small pond.

You must become a life long learner, move into the learning zone, and learn as much as you absolutely can. If you don't, you soon create the fixed mindset within yourself and begin to move in the opposite direction.

If you are not growing, you're dying.

I like to relate the mind to a gym. When you go to the gym, you lift weights and put massive amounts of stress on your muscles, in order for them to grow. If you do not stress your muscles, they will not grow. If you do the same routine every day, your muscles will stop growing because they are not being stressed anymore.

The exact same thing is true for your mind. If you are not uncomfortable, you are not growing. If you stay in the same routine every day, your mind gets used to it and ceases to grow. As with muscles, your mind will actually start to deteriorate if it is not used and challenged frequently. So feel comfort (oh the irony) in the fact that when you are stressed, uncomfortable, or feel vulnerable, you are actually growing your mind.

It is not enough to learn something, accomplish something, and then go on autopilot. You must be feverishly challenging your mind. The trick of this key is to practice "Constant Renewal." Master a skill, then keep learning.

This key is especially important for you as the entrepreneur. In almost every stage of business building, there is so much that we don't know and must learn. As entrepreneurs we are pushed off a cliff and must learn to build the plane on the way down. If we can check our egos and ask for help, we will learn ten times faster than trying on our own. This key has saved me from disaster many times in business. If had too much of an ego to ask for help, I would not be writing this book today. Once you come to the conclusion that you don't know it all and must continue to learn forever, you will be able to achieve more than you ever thought possible in your business.

As Napoleon Hill says,

"Whatever the mind can conceive and believe,
it can achieve."

We can continue to grow in every aspect of our lives; we can continue to strengthen the keys to breaking our limiting beliefs:

GROWTH IN WHY

You must challenge your beliefs continuously so that they may grow with you.

Marc Andreesen uses the phrase, **"Strong views, loosely held."** This means that you need to have strong conviction in your ideas and beliefs, but when the world changes, or when better information presents itself, admit it.

As you grow in your life, your values and goals should grow as well. This isn't a cause for concern but is a natural progression. The worse scenario is someone who blindly follows old values and small goals even when new information has presented itself. This is the opposite of growth.

GROWTH FROM FAILURES

Failure is arguably the best time to grow. People rarely learn anything from success. But when you fail, it challenges you to look in the mirror and examine the causes. It challenges you to become better. People without limiting beliefs and successful entrepreneurs understand that failure is a part of life that should not be avoided, but embraced. It is a step on the journey to success, as long as we let it be. In order to use failure to your advantage, you must learn from it. You must grow from it.

GROWTH IN HABITS

You can use your habits to grow instead of using them to become stagnant. You can create habits of reading, journaling, exercising, or meditating. You can create habits that assist you in growing. Ultimately you can create a habit of constant growth in every aspect of your life.

GROWTH IN PEOPLE

By selecting the right people, you can grow from everyone you associate with. You can find accountability partners, mentors, and teammates who push you to grow further than you ever thought possible, resulting in your business growing further than you imagined. You can have role models that inspire you to be better and grow more. Benjamin Franklin used his Junto groups (a group of associates who met regularly) to force his growth. You can do the same.

CHALLENGES

1. Learn a new concept every day for a week. You can do this by talking to people, reading a book, or just researching on the internet.

2. Actively attempt to learn and remember everyone's name that you come into contact with. A good tip for this is to say their name back to them three times in the first five minutes of conversation. "Hi, my name is John." "Hey,

John! My name is Christian. So what do you do, John?"
etc... This will imprint their name in your mind. This strengthens your memory and makes you a lot more likeable with new people.

CHAPTER RECAP:

1. The fifth and final key is Growth

2. Check your ego at the door and realize you have so much to learn

3. Socrates said **"I know one thing: that I know nothing"**

4. The only way to truly learn all the time is to get out of your comfort zone and into the learning zone.

5. You are only growing your body when it is stressed and uncomfortable, the same goes for your mind.

6. Constant growth is a must for success in business.

7. You can use the key of growth to maximize the other four keys

CHAPTER TOOLS

Think back to a time when you turned down someone teaching you something just because you didn't want to seem stupid. Why did you do this?

Write down 3 specific areas you should focus your growth in? For business it could be leadership, sales, management, accounting, etc. For personal it could be organization, mediation, nutrition, exercise, etc.)

What can you do today to get out of your comfort zone? Write down 3 ideas.

What skills do you need to learn to dramatically increase the success of your business? Do you know someone you can ask to teach you these skills?

NO WHAT IF'S

*"Two roads diverged in a wood,
and I – I took the one less traveled by,
And that has made all the difference."*

Whatever your limiting beliefs are, it is now time to Lose your Limits.

Whatever business you are struggling to grow, it is now time to Grow your Business.

The quote above has guided me my entire life. My mother used to read the quote to me every night before bed. It is the reason I am where I am today.

According to the Social Security Administration, if you take any 100 people and track their life until retirement, you will find that:

- 5 people will continue working past retirement, not because they want to but because they have to.
- 36 will be dead.

- 54 will be broke and dependent on friends, family, and the government to take care of them.
- 4 will be financially secure.
- Only 1 will be wealthy.

This means only 5 out of 100 people will be living the life entrepreneurs like you strive for.

Only 5% of us achieve success and freedom, monetarily speaking. The other 95% will struggle their entire lives.

It is extremely hard to take a different path in life. I know this, and you know this. By buying this book and reading it, though, you at least realize that you are not exactly where you want to be. So you are ahead of 95% of the world. Most people will die in the same exact place they were born, and that is very sad.

Steve Jobs, the late Apple founder, illuminates this issue with the following words:

> "When you grow up you tend to get told the world is the way it is and your life is just to live your life inside the world.
>
> Try not to bash into the walls too much. Try to have a nice family, have fun, save a little money.
>
> That's a very limited life.
>
> Life can be much broader once you discover one simple fact:

Everything around you that you call life was made up by people that were no smarter than you and you can change it, you can influence it, you can build your own things that other people can use.

Once you learn that, you'll never be the same again."

It is not enough to just read this book. You must now take action. I urge you to use these five keys and challenge social conventions. Grab a pen and paper **right now** and get to work on creating an action plan for implementing the keys. They are nothing without action. They require you to make changes in your life; to think more differently than you ever have. The keys will help you, like Steve Jobs says, change the world around you, influence the world around you, and build your own things.

I promise you, if you do your absolute best, reflect on your choices, and consistently keep the keys in your mind, you will see a drastic difference in your life and in your business.

So, my last Challenge to you is this: break your limiting beliefs, grow your business, and take the road less traveled.

The 5 keys to go from struggling business owner
to limitless entrepreneur.

KEY 1: WHY

KEY 2: FAILURE

KEY 3: HABIT

KEY 4: PEOPLE

KEY 5: GROWTH

QUOTES TO GUIDE YOU:

"Beliefs have the power to create and the power to destroy."
— TONY ROBBINS

"If you want to be something more than just average, you must delve into the idea of being uncomfortable."
— JARRET GROSSMAN

"All that we are is a result of what we have thought."
— BUDDHA

"What we can or cannot do, what we consider possible or impossible, is rarely a function of our true capability. It is more likely a function of our beliefs about who we are."
— TONY ROBBINS

"

*"If you do what everyone else does, you will wind
up having what everyone else has."*
– ROBERT KIYOSAKI

*"Effort only fully releases its reward after
a person refuses to quit."*
– NAPOLEON HILL

*"Our levels of success will rarely exceed
our level of personal development. Because success is
something we attract by who we become."*
– JIM ROHN

*"If you want your life to be different, you have to
be willing to do something different first."*
– UNKNOWN

ADDITIONAL TOOLS

For video trainings, tools, and coaching for breaking your limiting beliefs and implementing the systems you need to scale your business to massive proportions, head over to losethelimits.com.

Sign up for Christian's newsletter to receive monthly blog posts, free education content, and more.

PAY IT FORWARD

If you took anything away from this book, please give this book to someone else who may gain some value.

ABOUT THE AUTHOR

Growing up in a small town in Southern New Jersey, Christian always had big dreams of making an impact in the world. He was frequently mentoring younger students and teammates and always loved being in a coaching role. He knew, though, that he needed to see the world and get out of his small town to truly make a difference in people's lives.

Christian is an entrepreneur who built two successful companies by the age of 25. While at the University of South Carolina, he built a franchise from $0 to $1.2 million in annual revenue. Now he co-owns a real estate investment company that has grown to $6.5 million revenue annually. He's also the author of the best-selling book Lose the Limits. The secret to his success lies in the systems he uses for both his personal life and his business. Sometimes success is accidental.But repeatable success is not.

Even in the short time Christian Chasmer has been an entrepreneur, he's proven that he can repeat his early success.

Christian now lives in San Diego where he continues to build CC Solutions while focusing on helping entrepreneurs implement the systems necessary to grow their business to massive proportions. He has a true passion for helping others optimize their lives.

If you have any comments, questions, or want to share success stories from using the five key system, email christian@losethelimits.com

82392893R00074

Made in the USA
Columbia, SC
16 December 2017